Tranquil.tangles@gmail.com

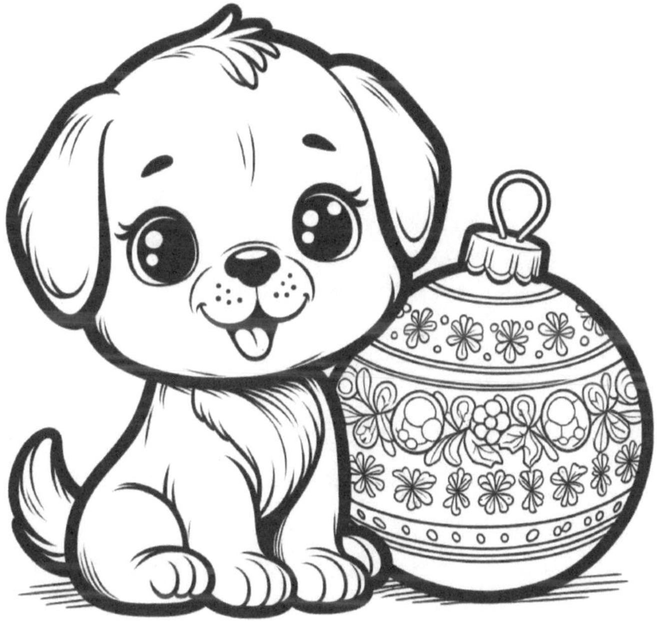

Color Test Page

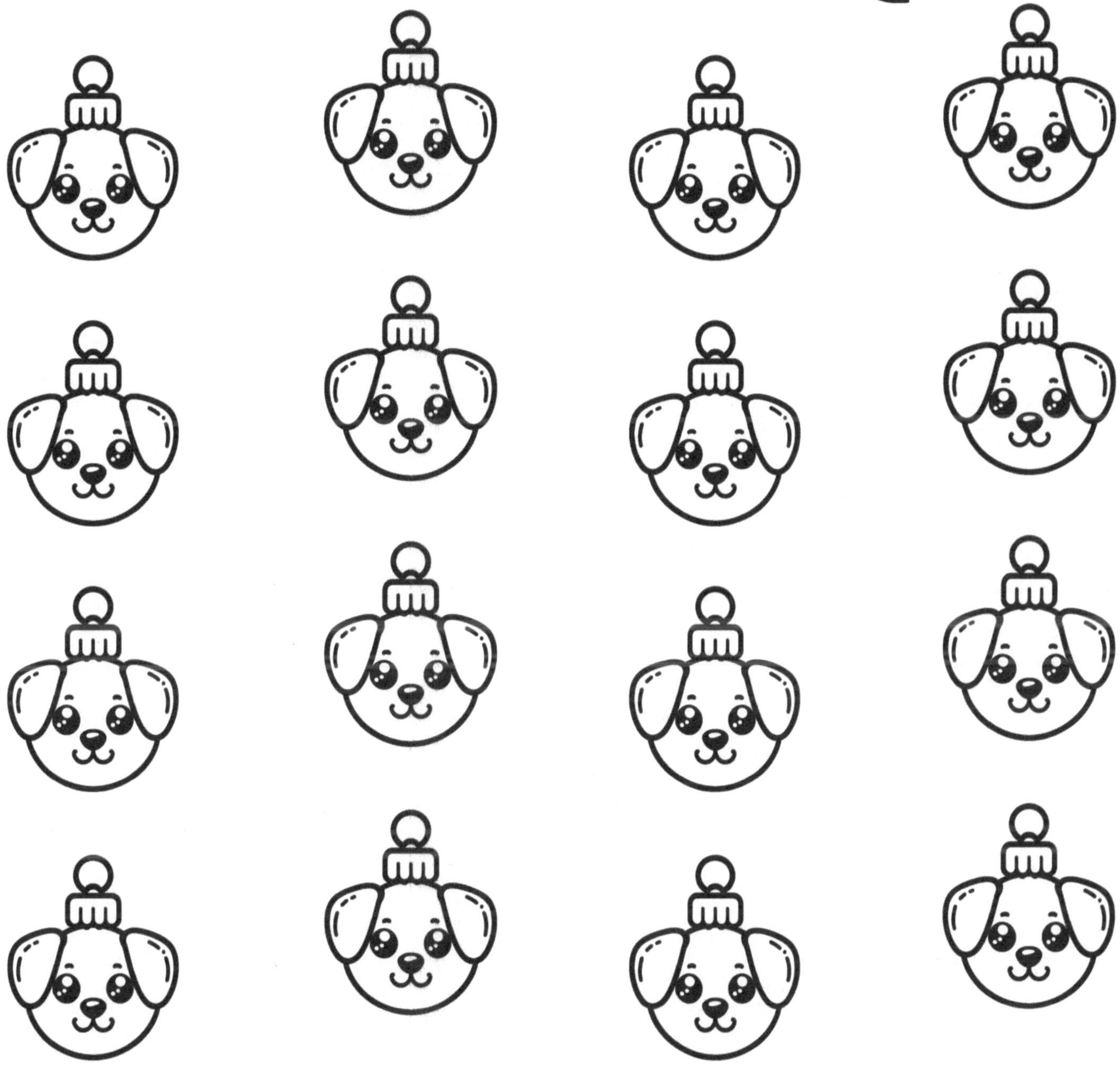

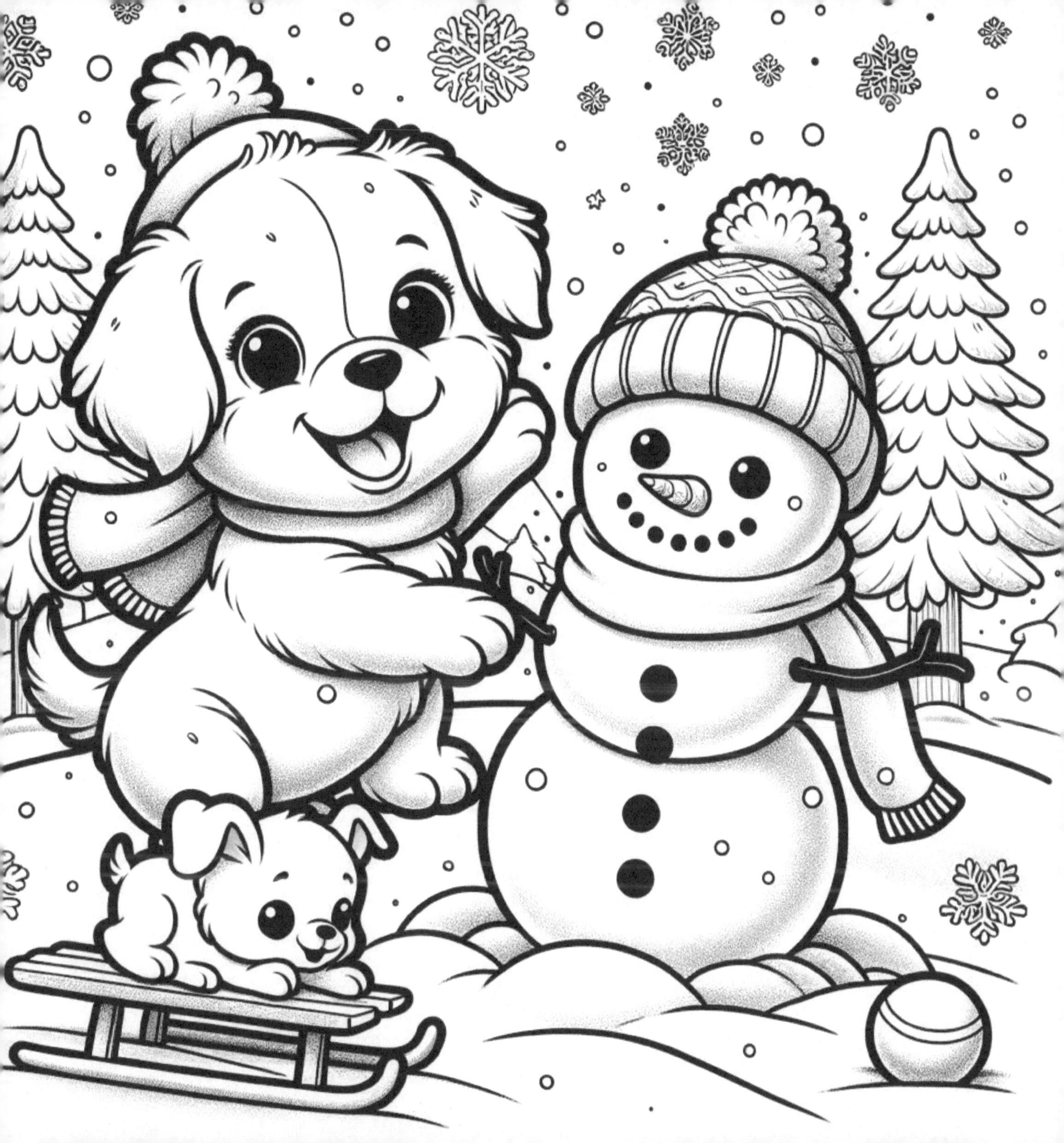

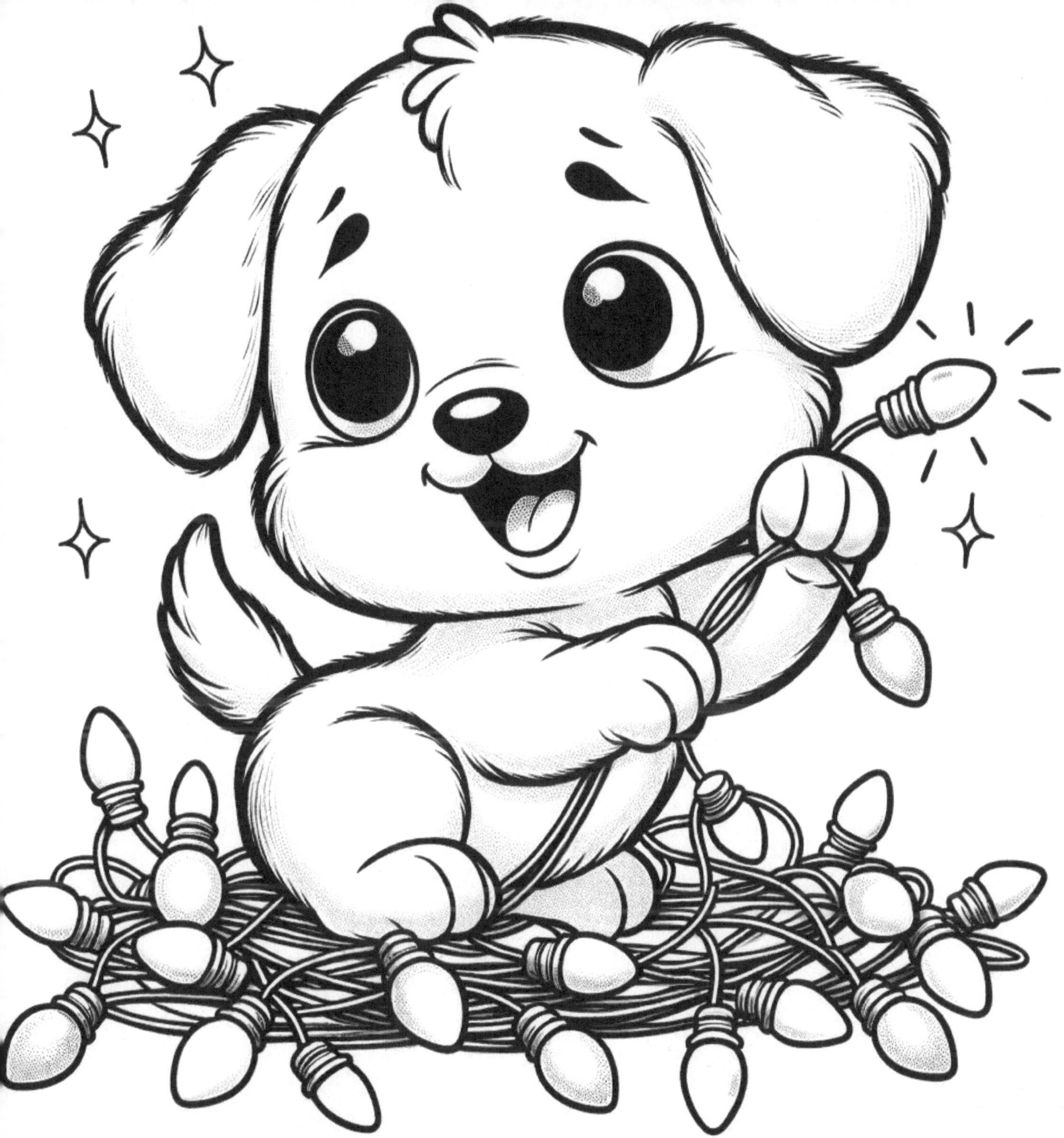

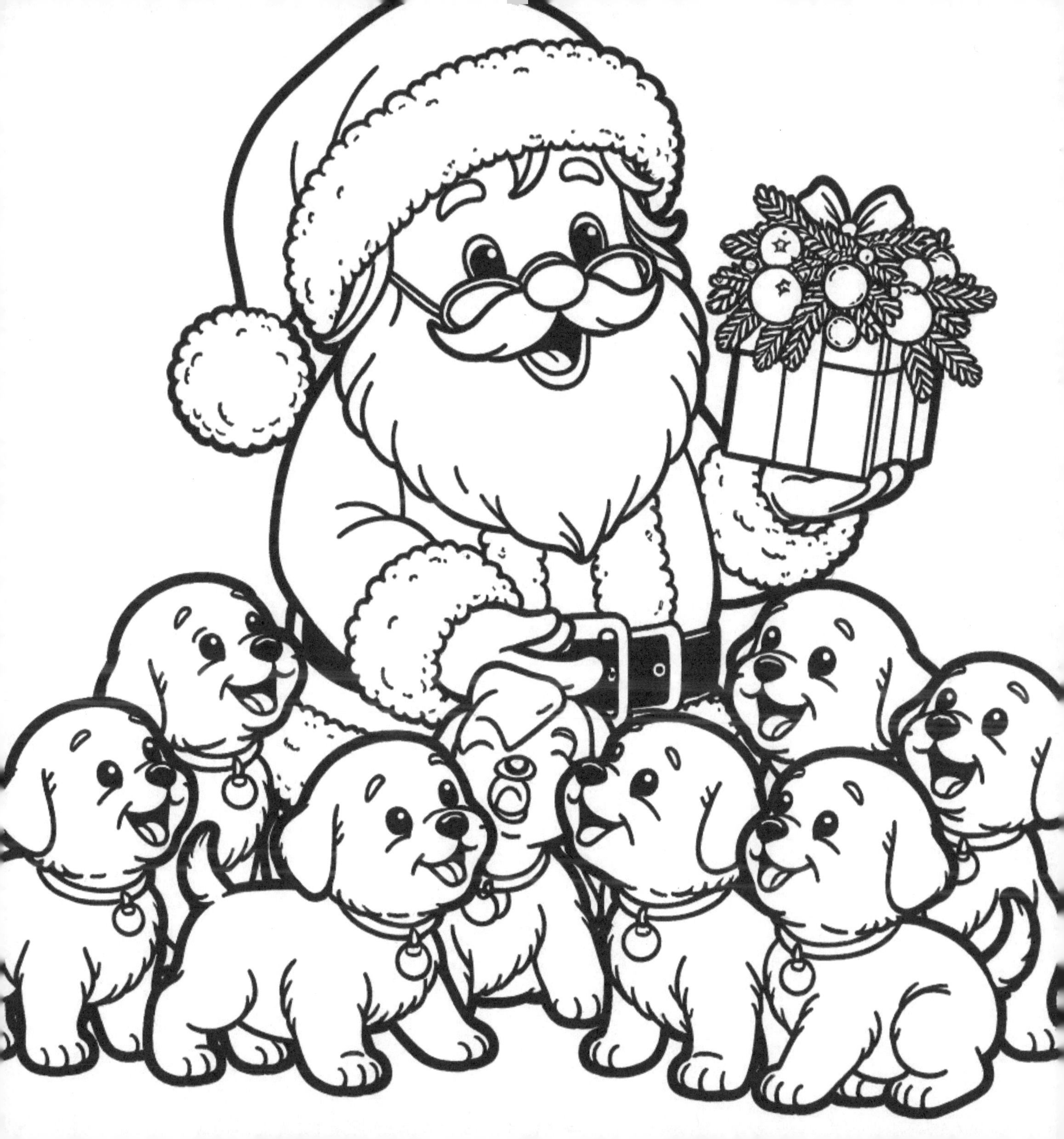

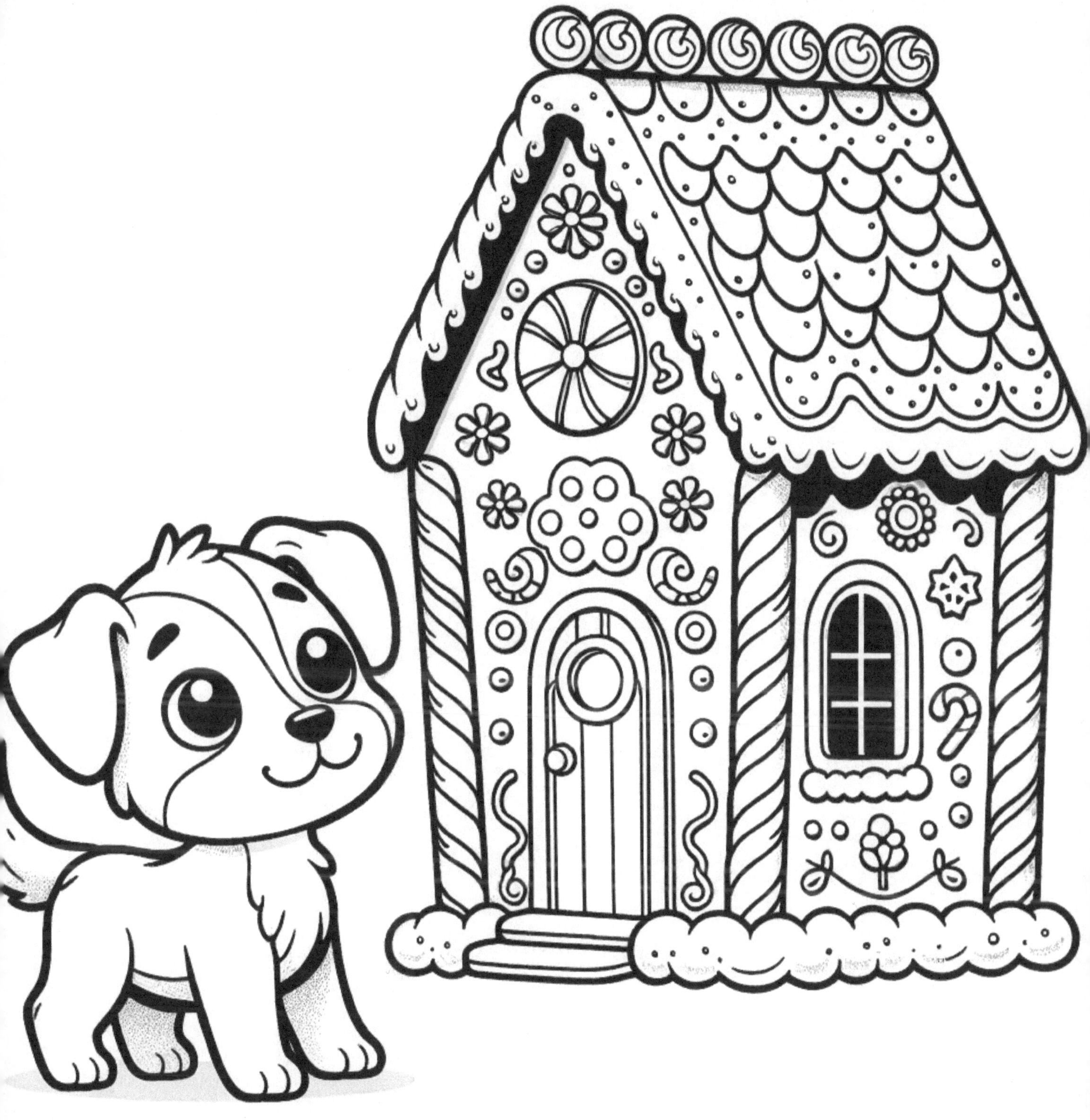

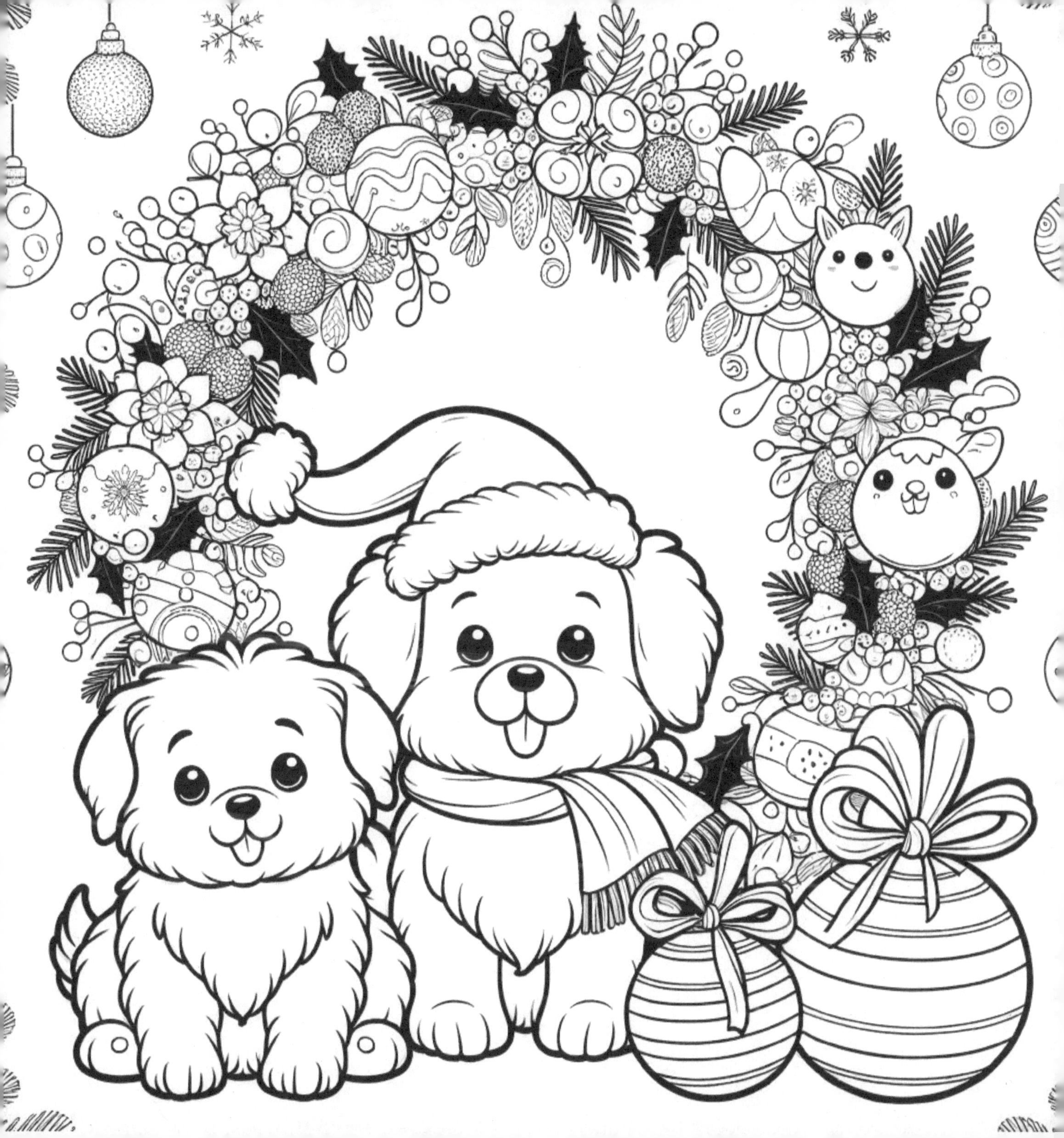

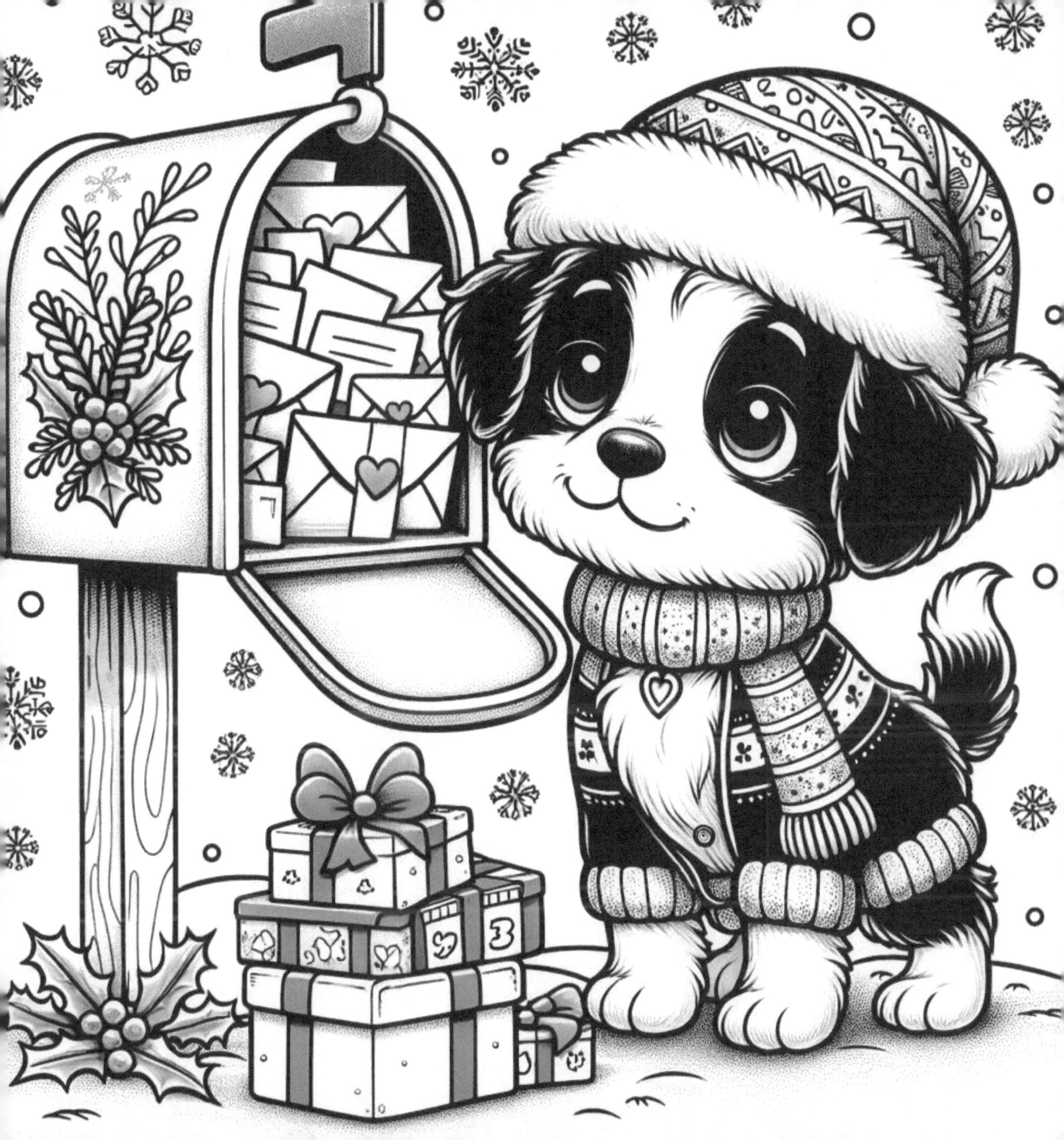

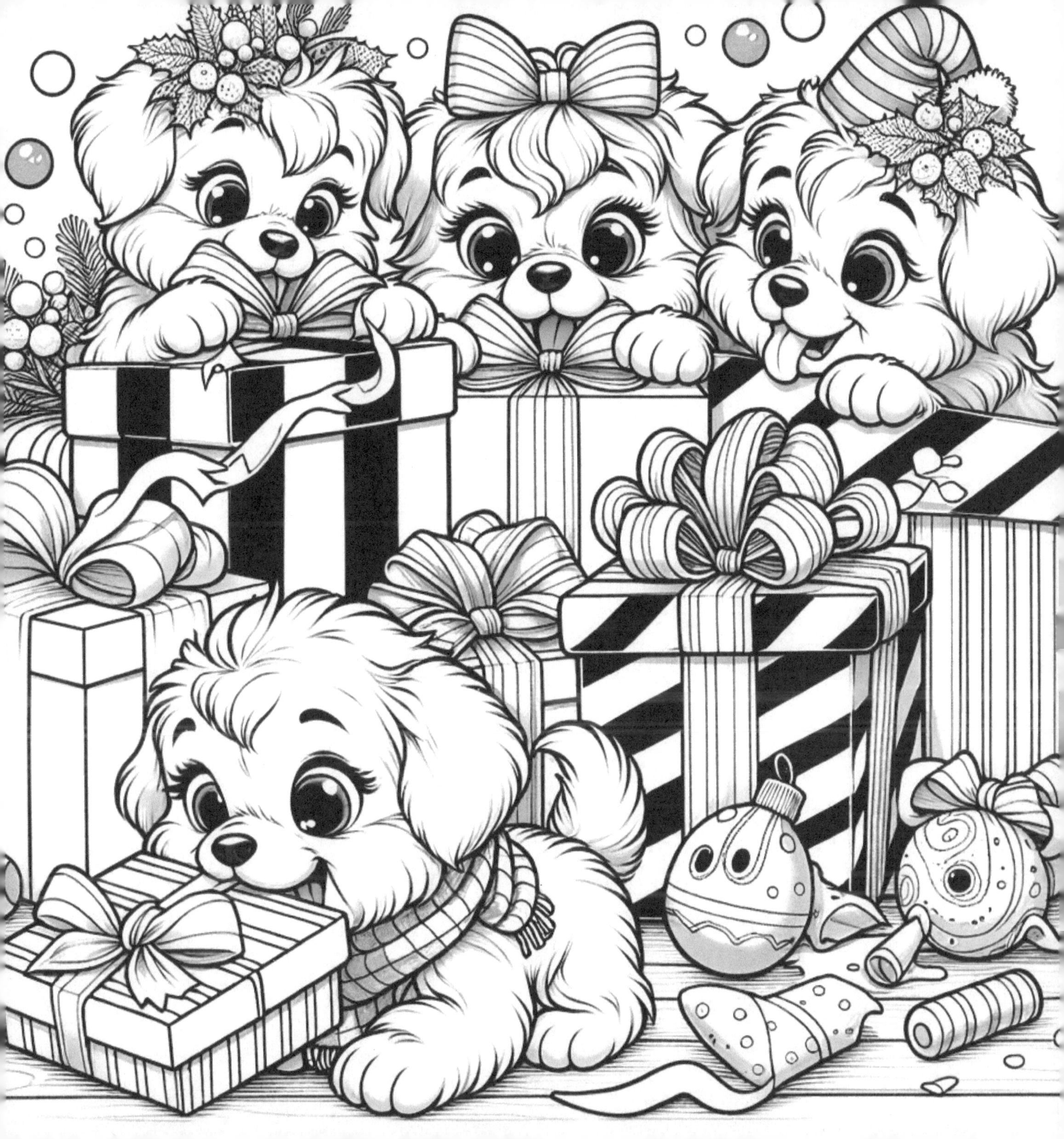

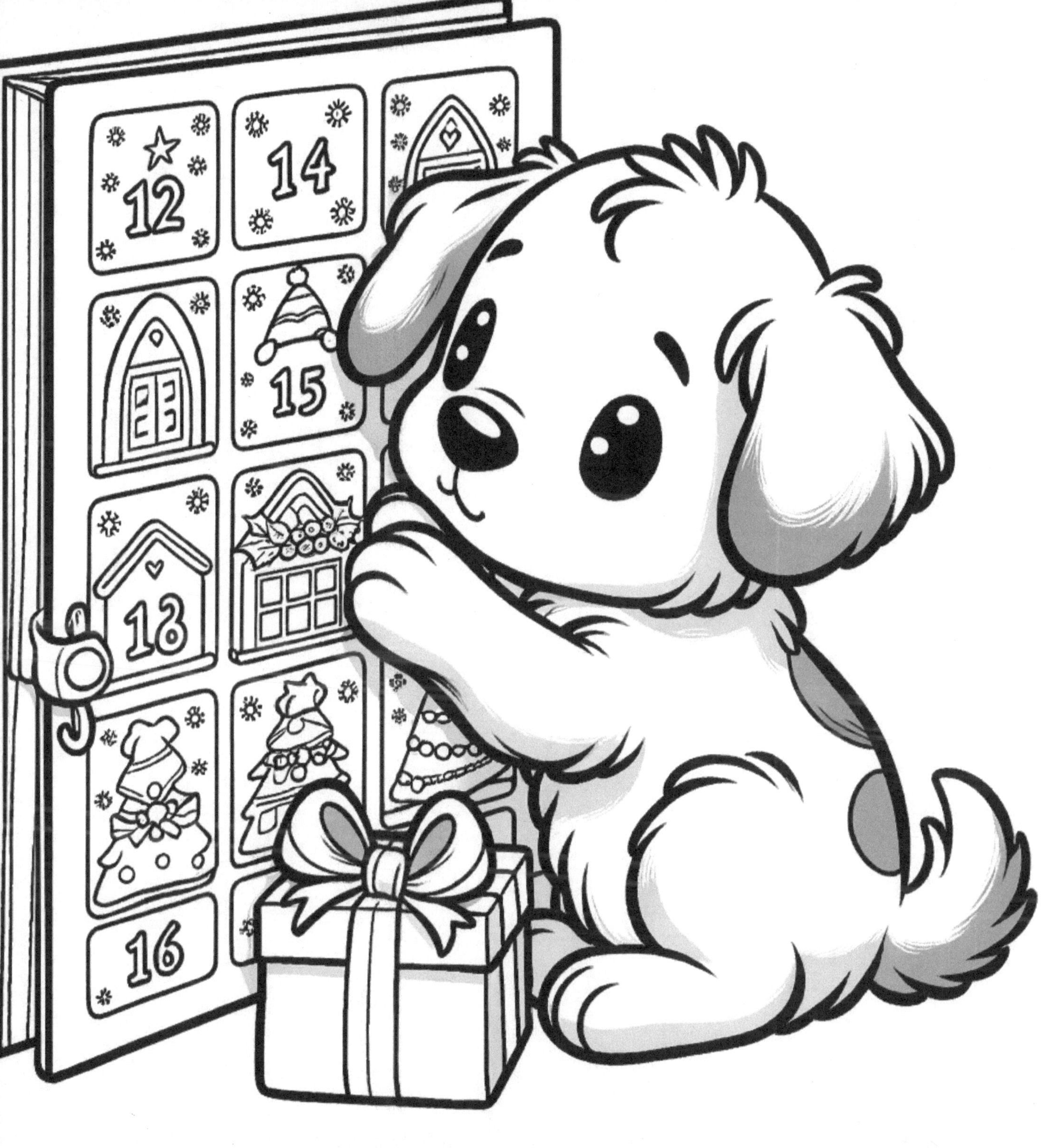
12
14
15
13
16

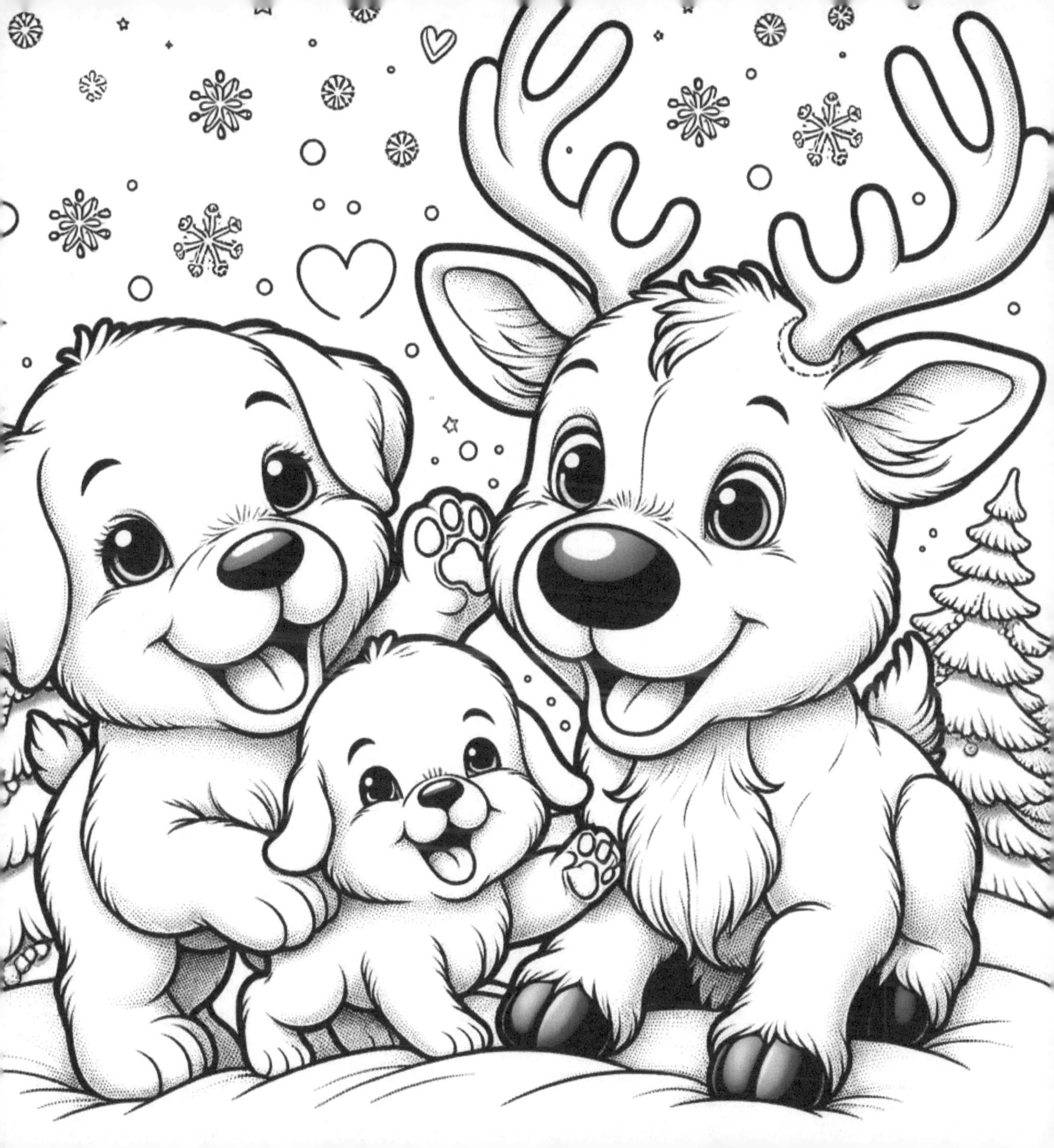

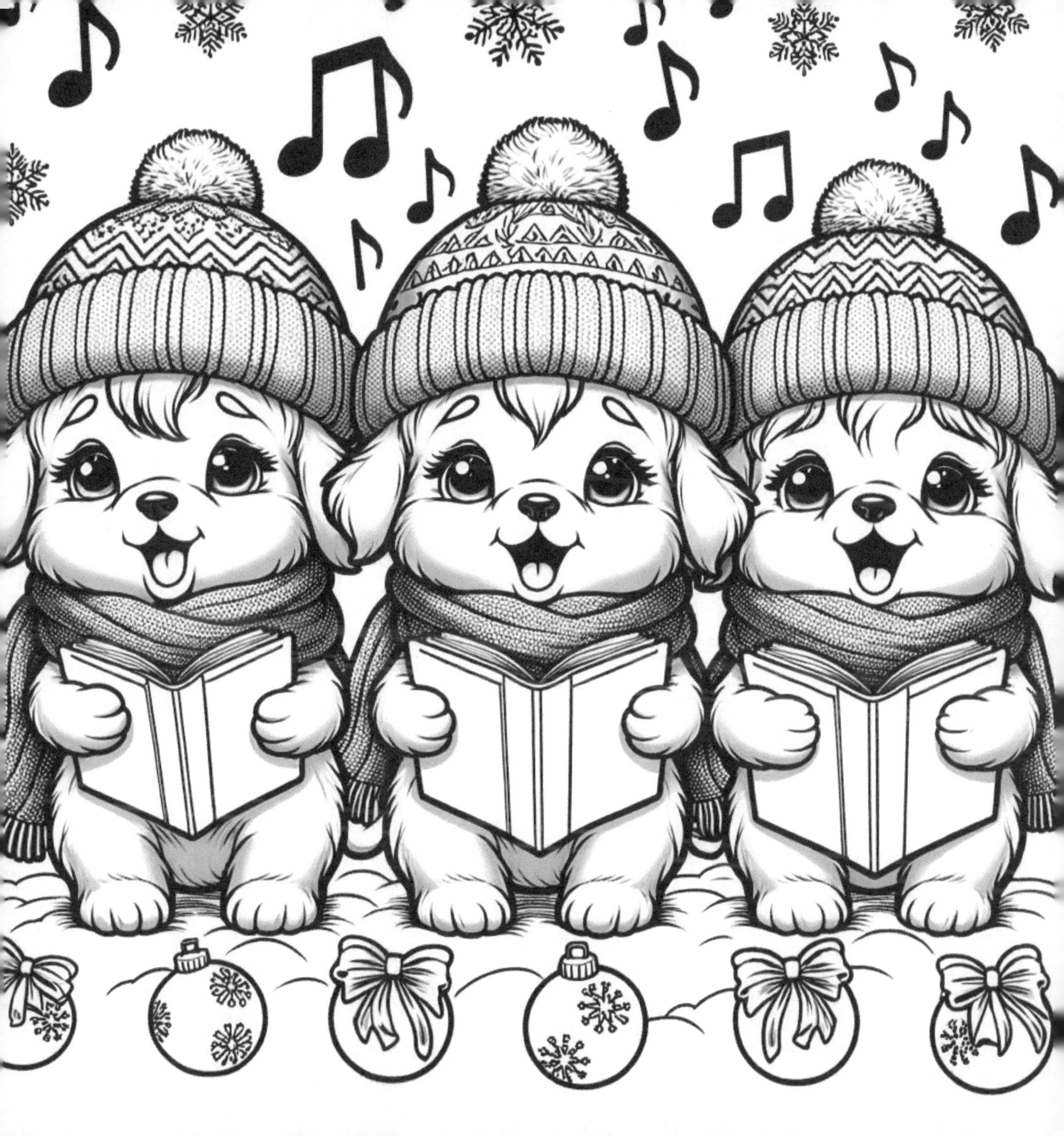

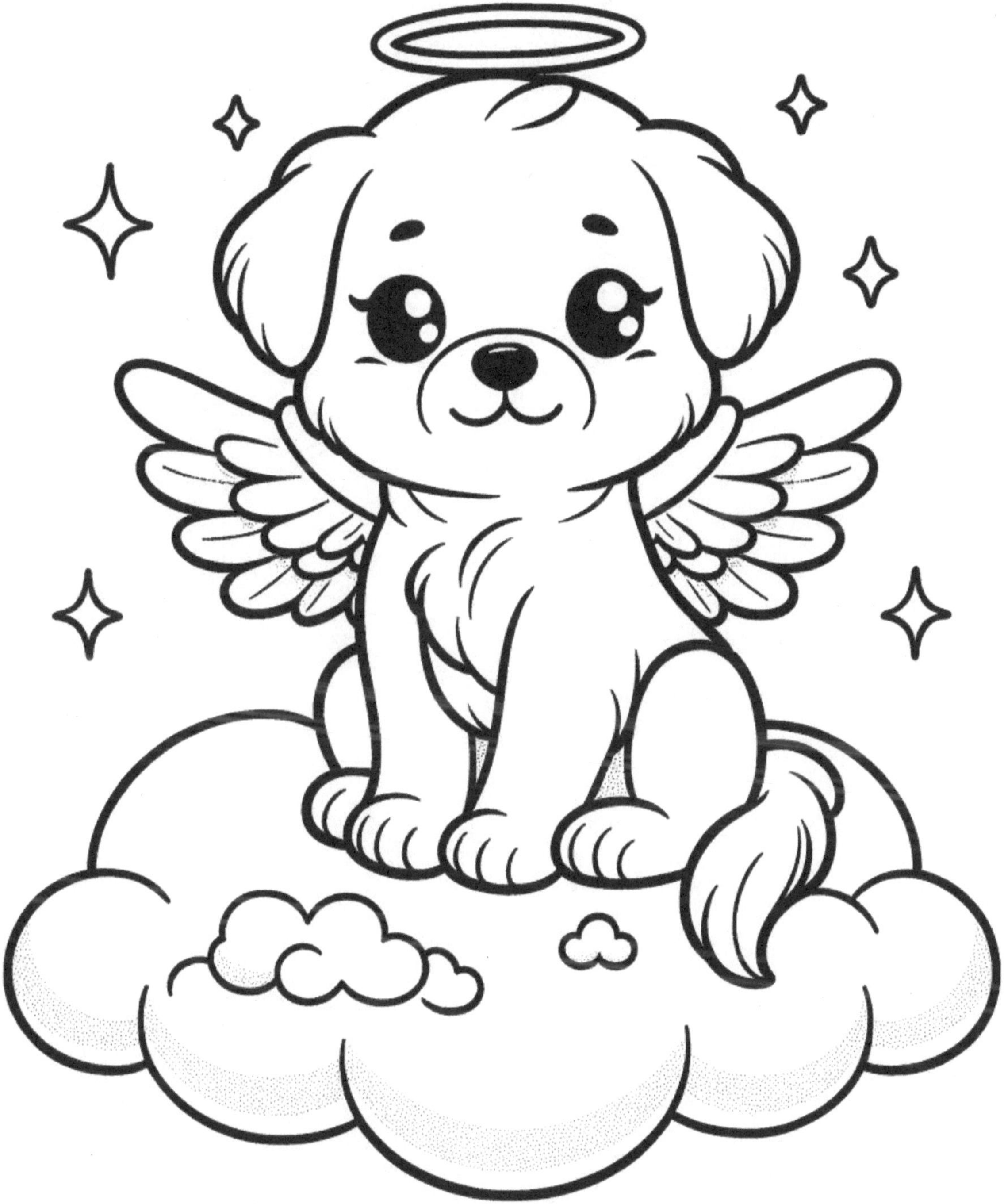

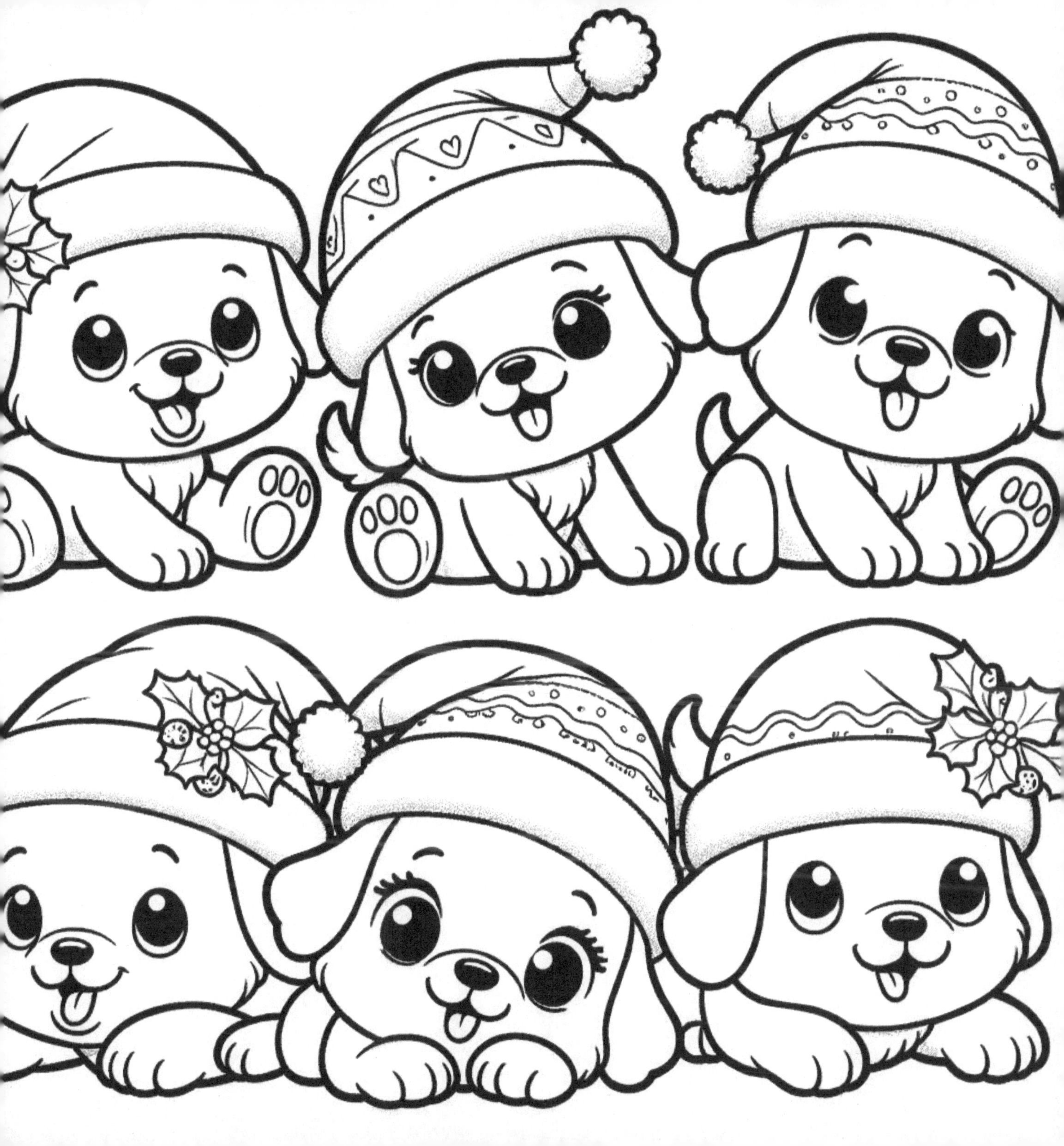

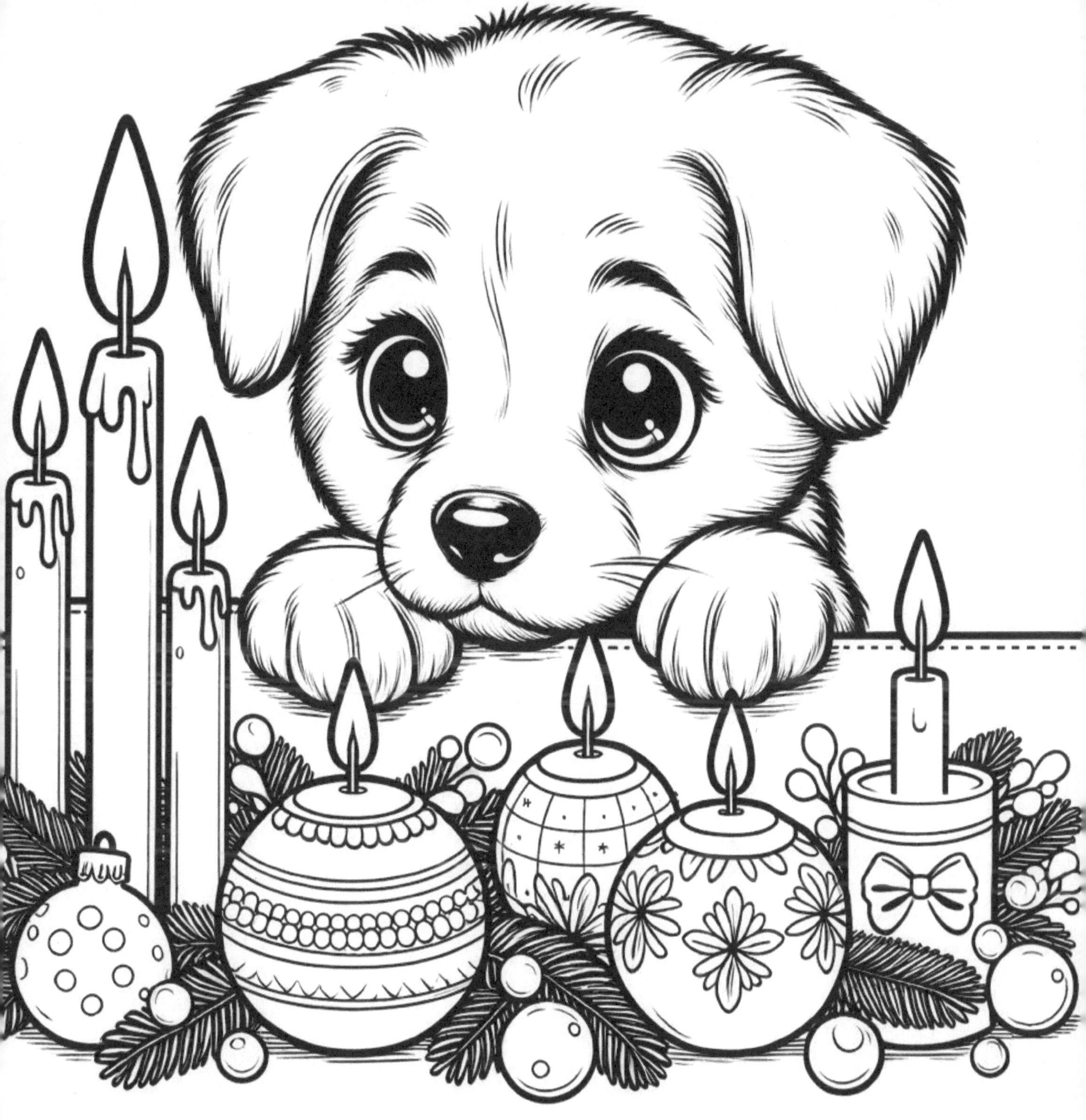

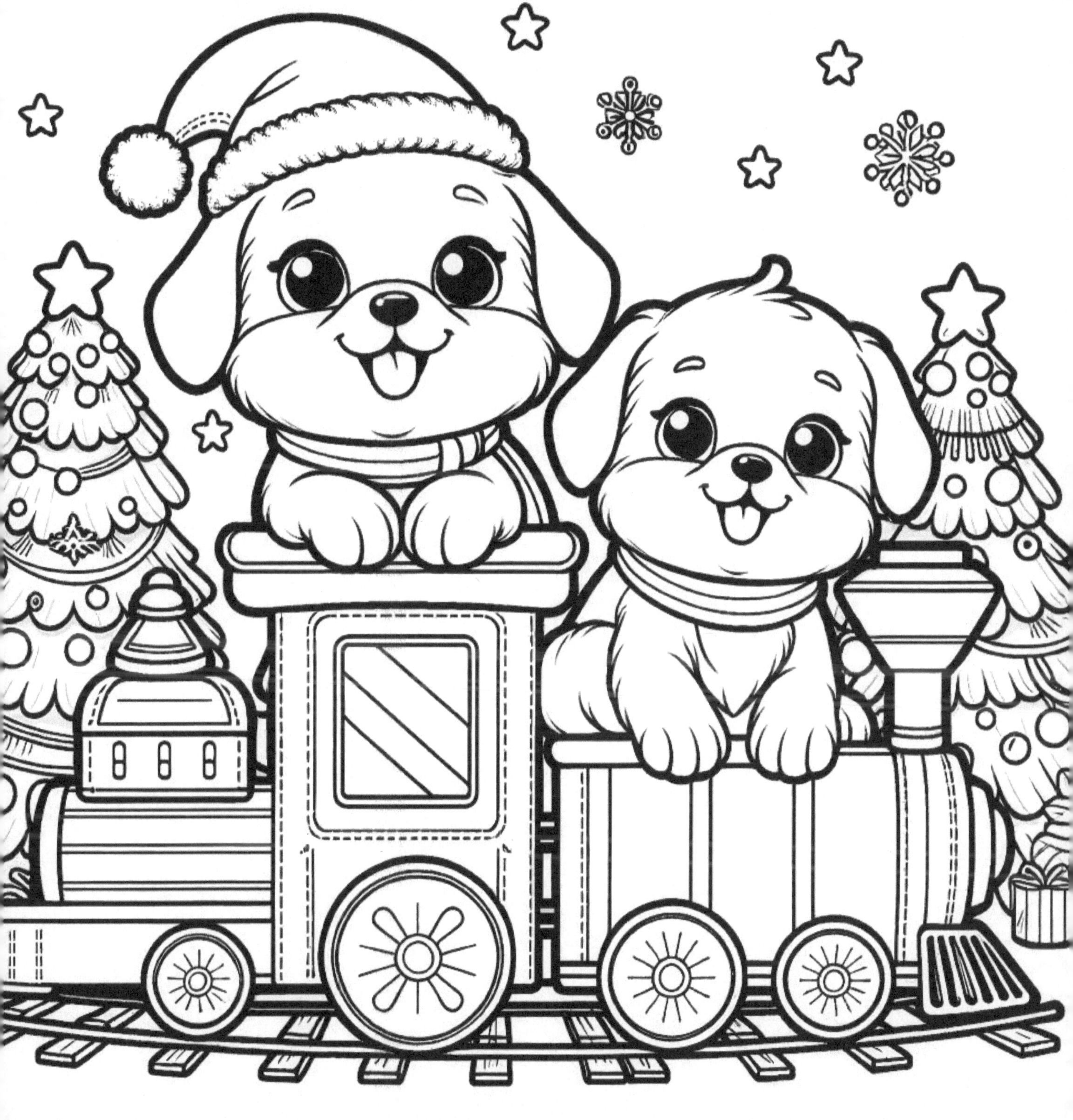

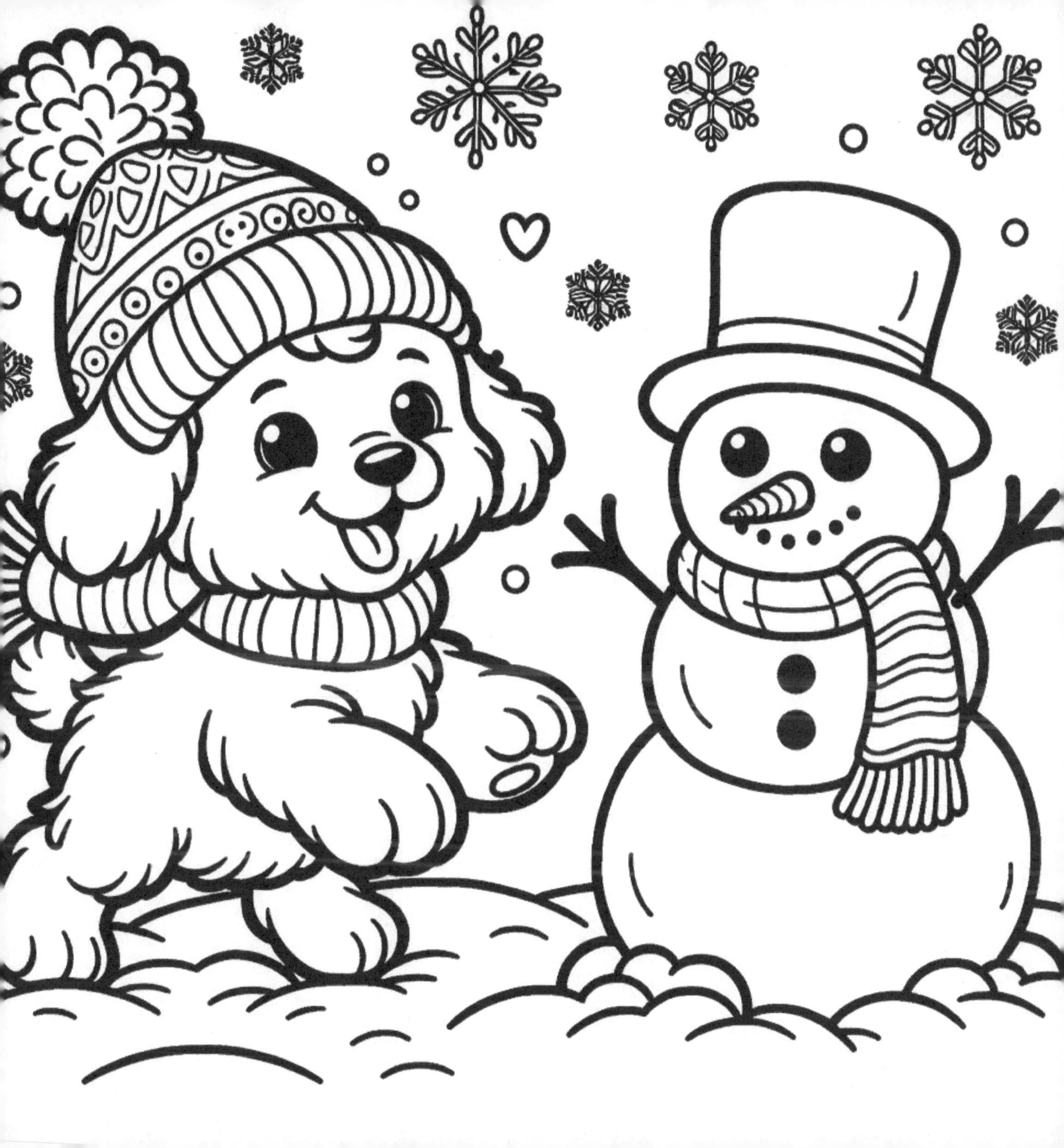

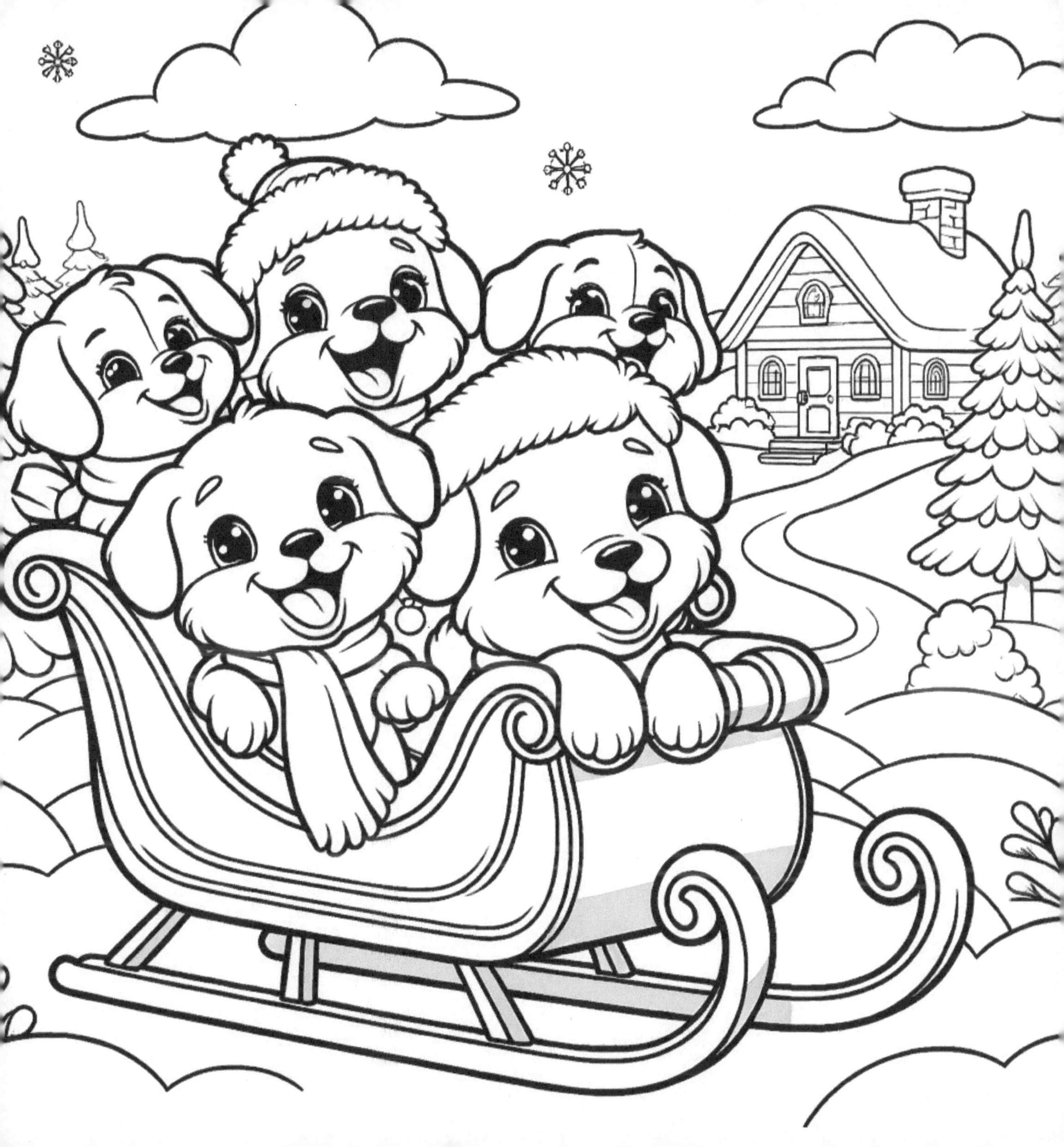

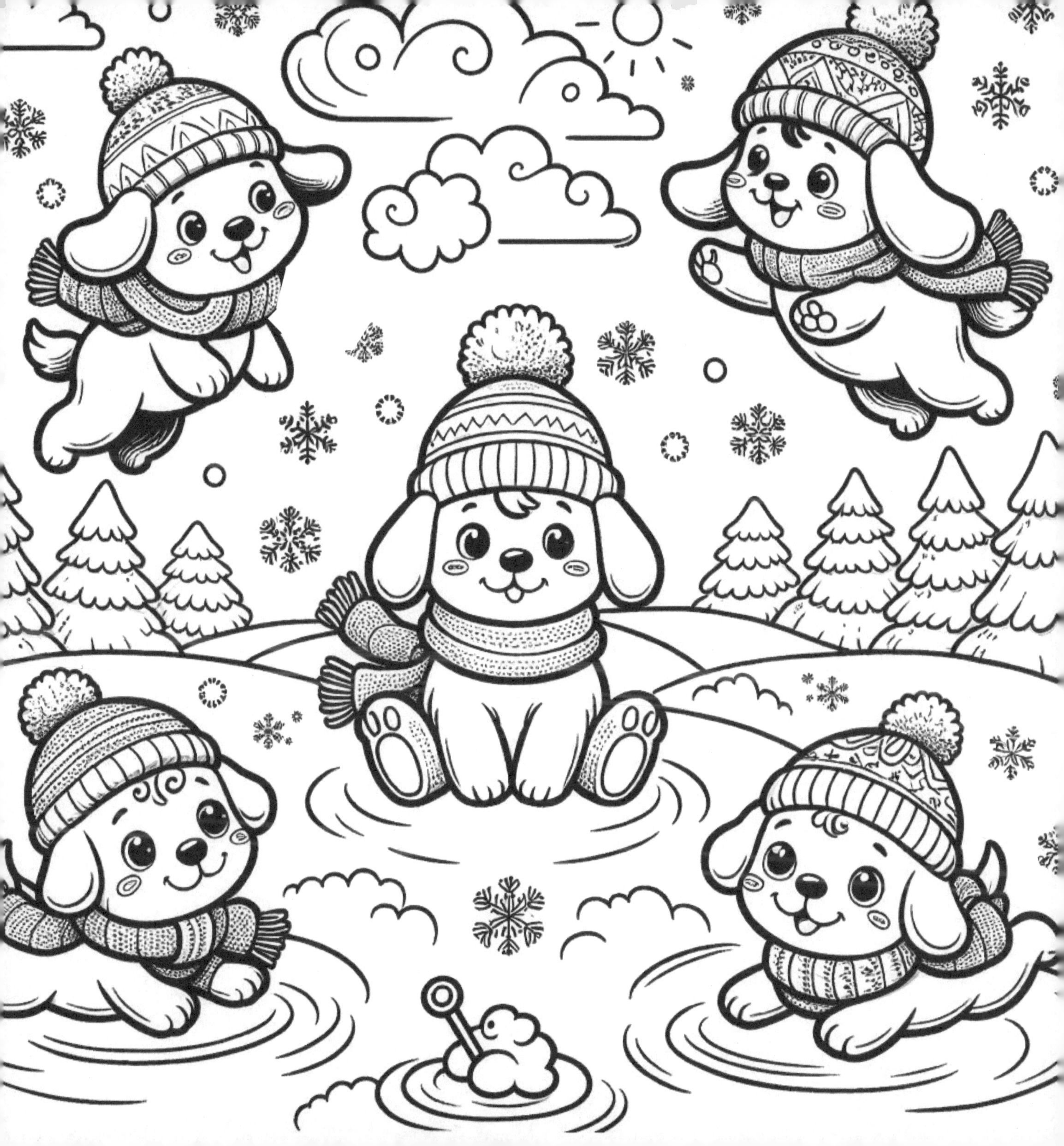

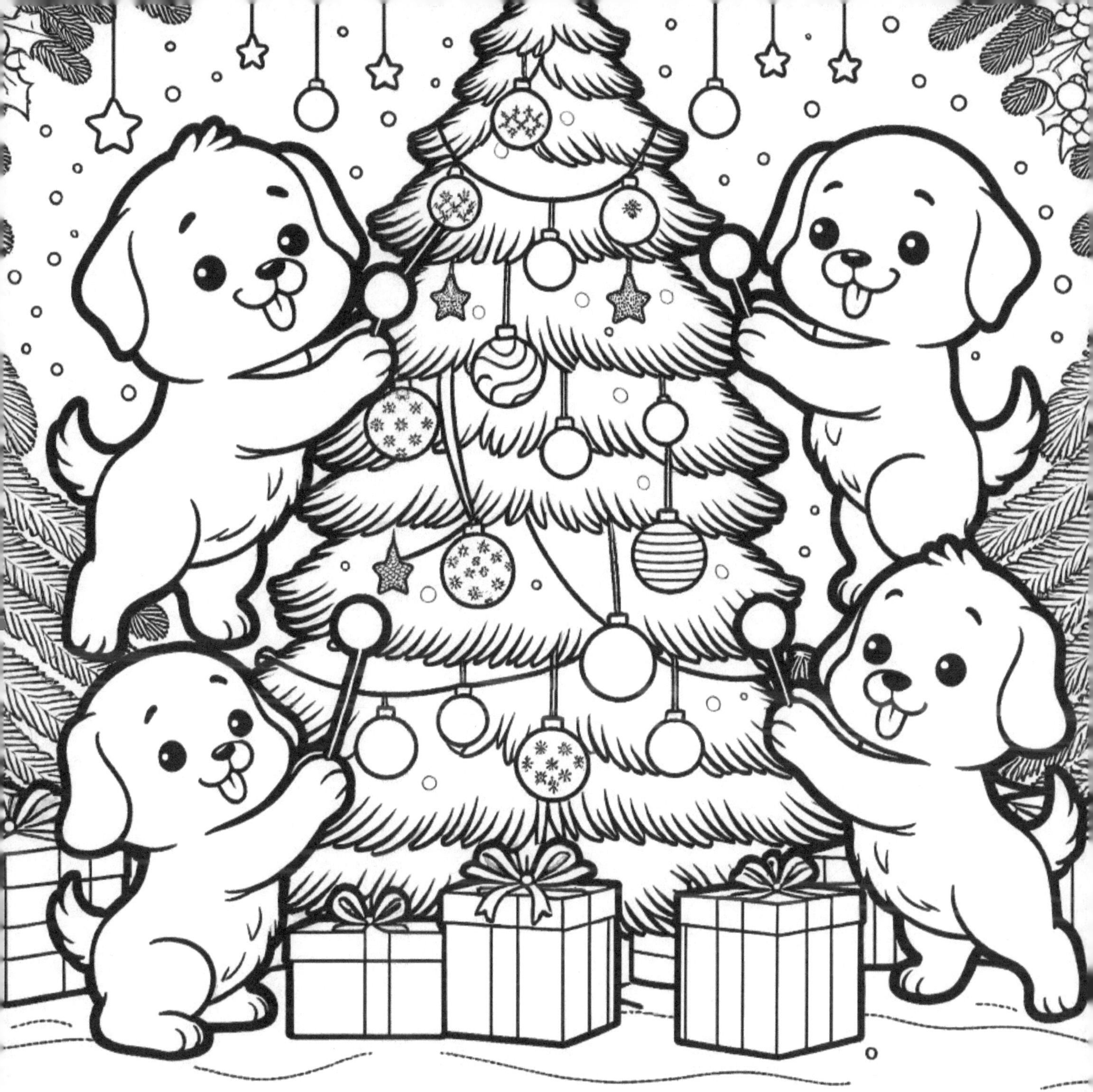

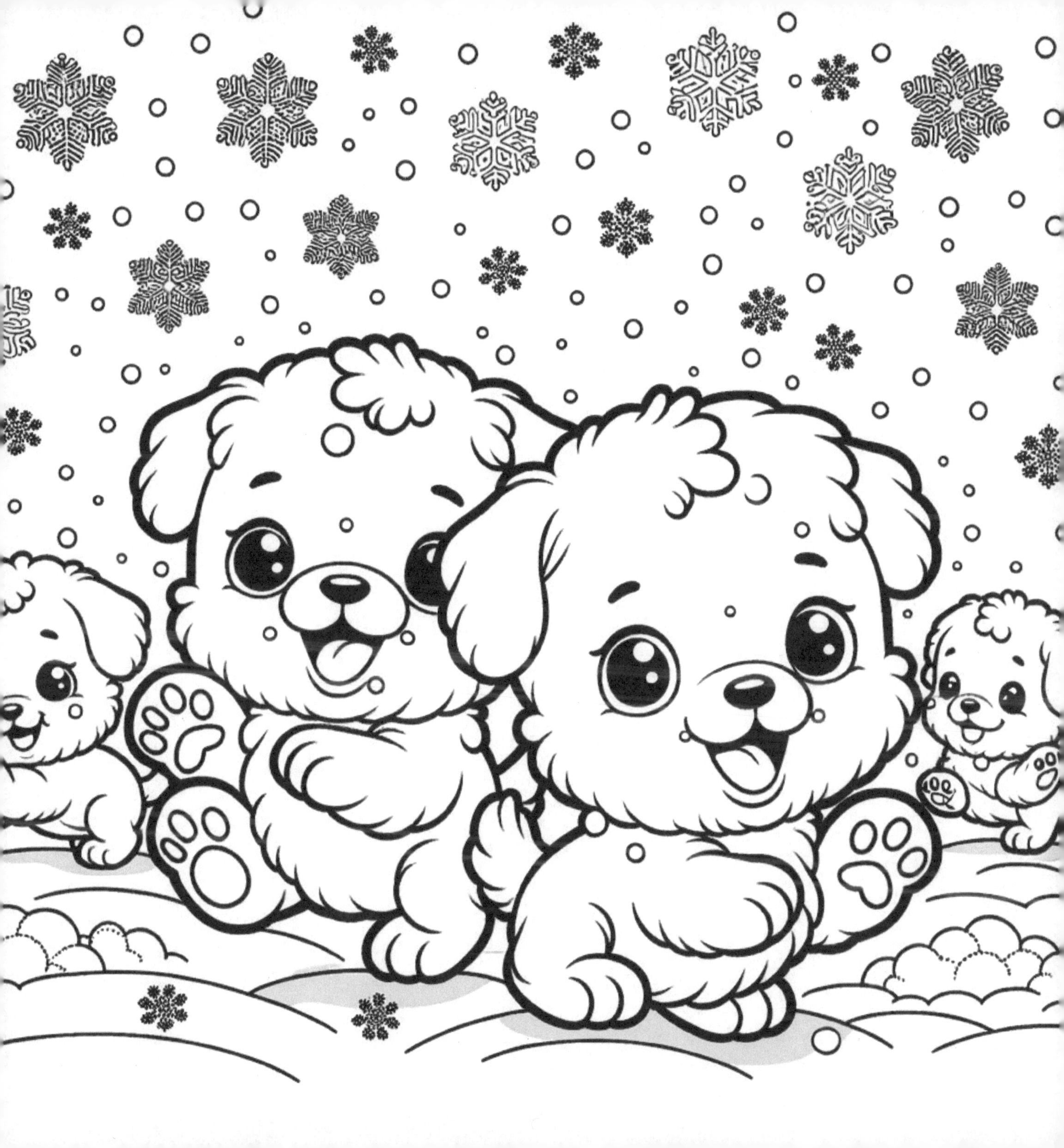

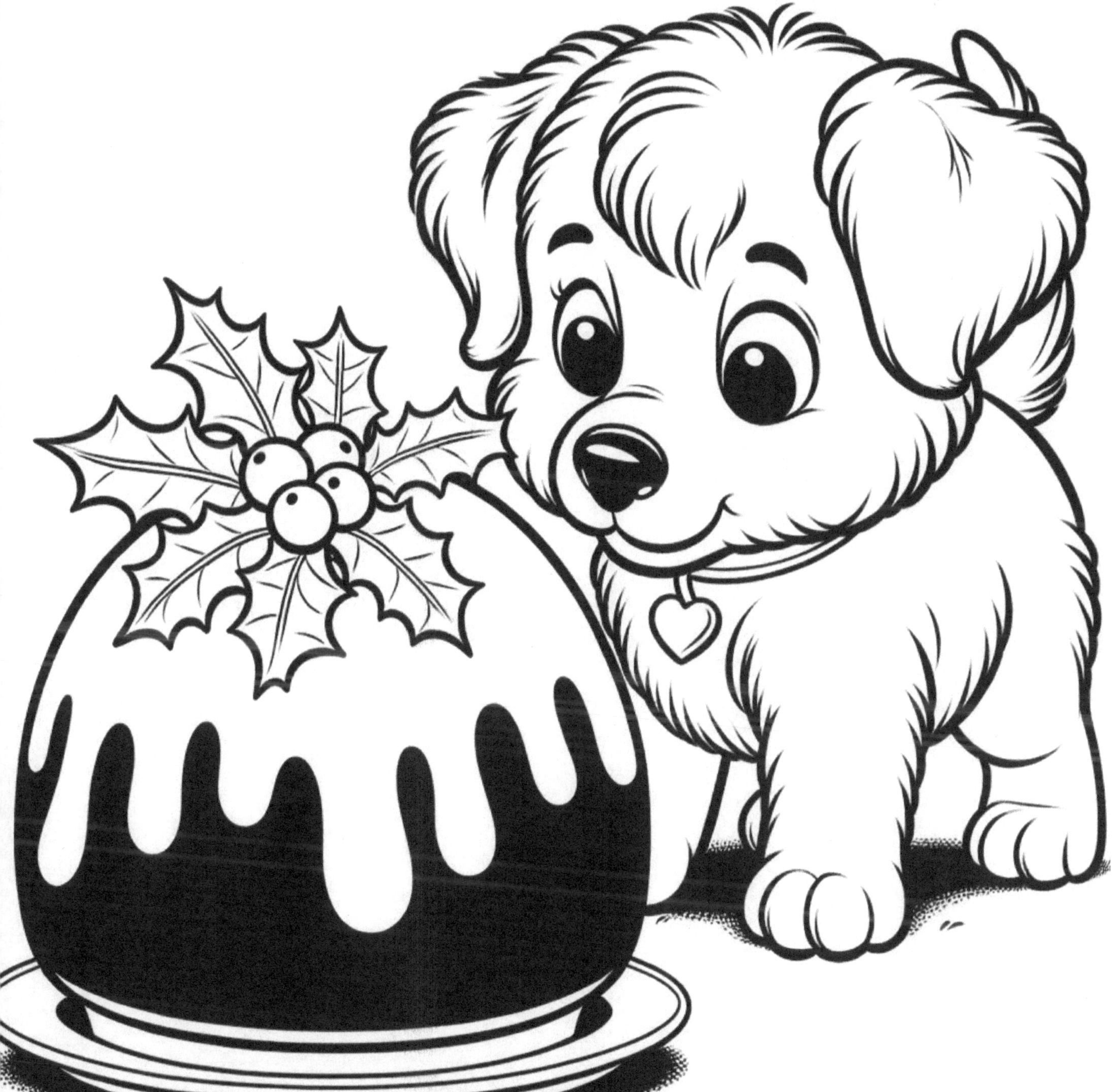

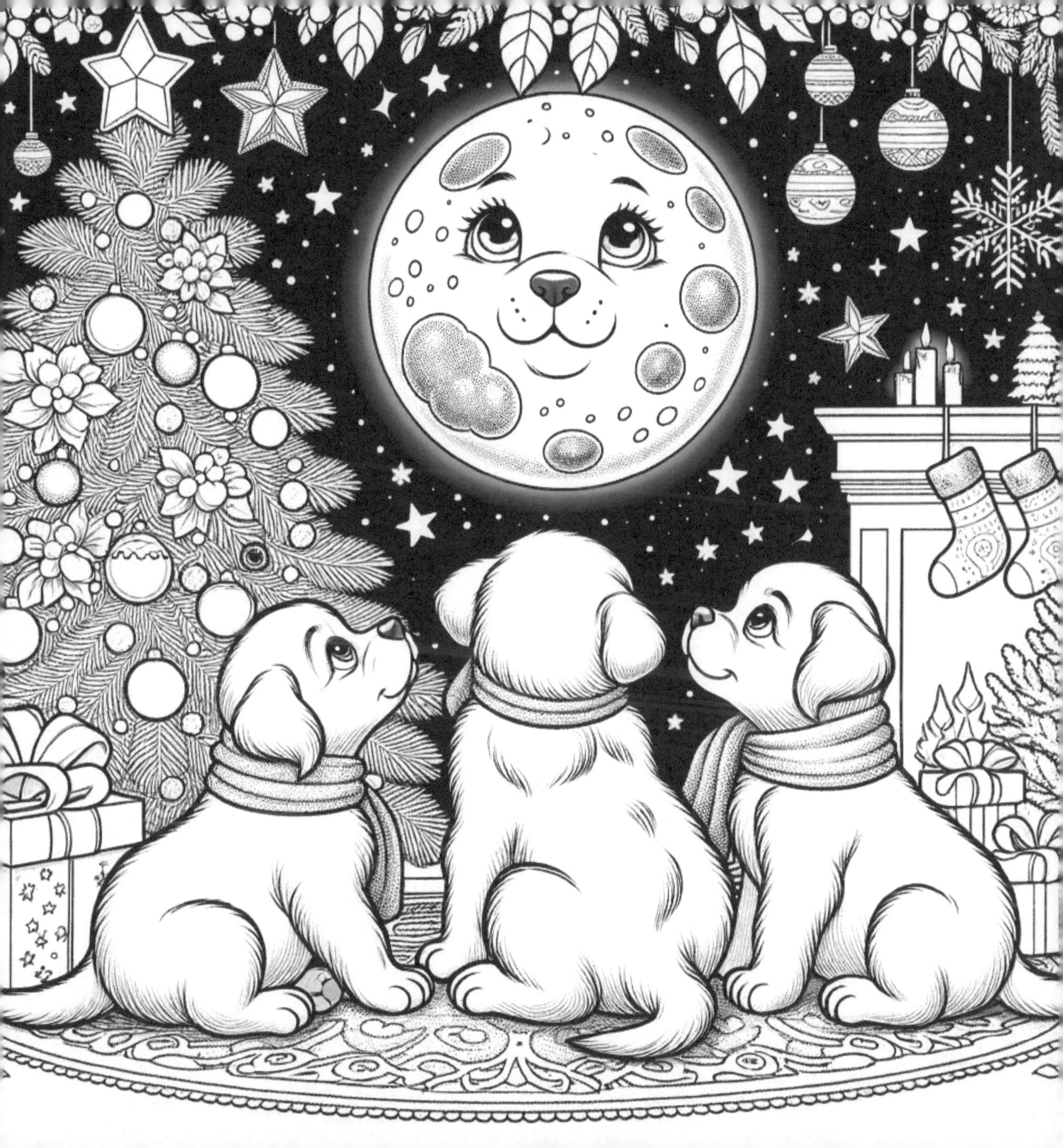

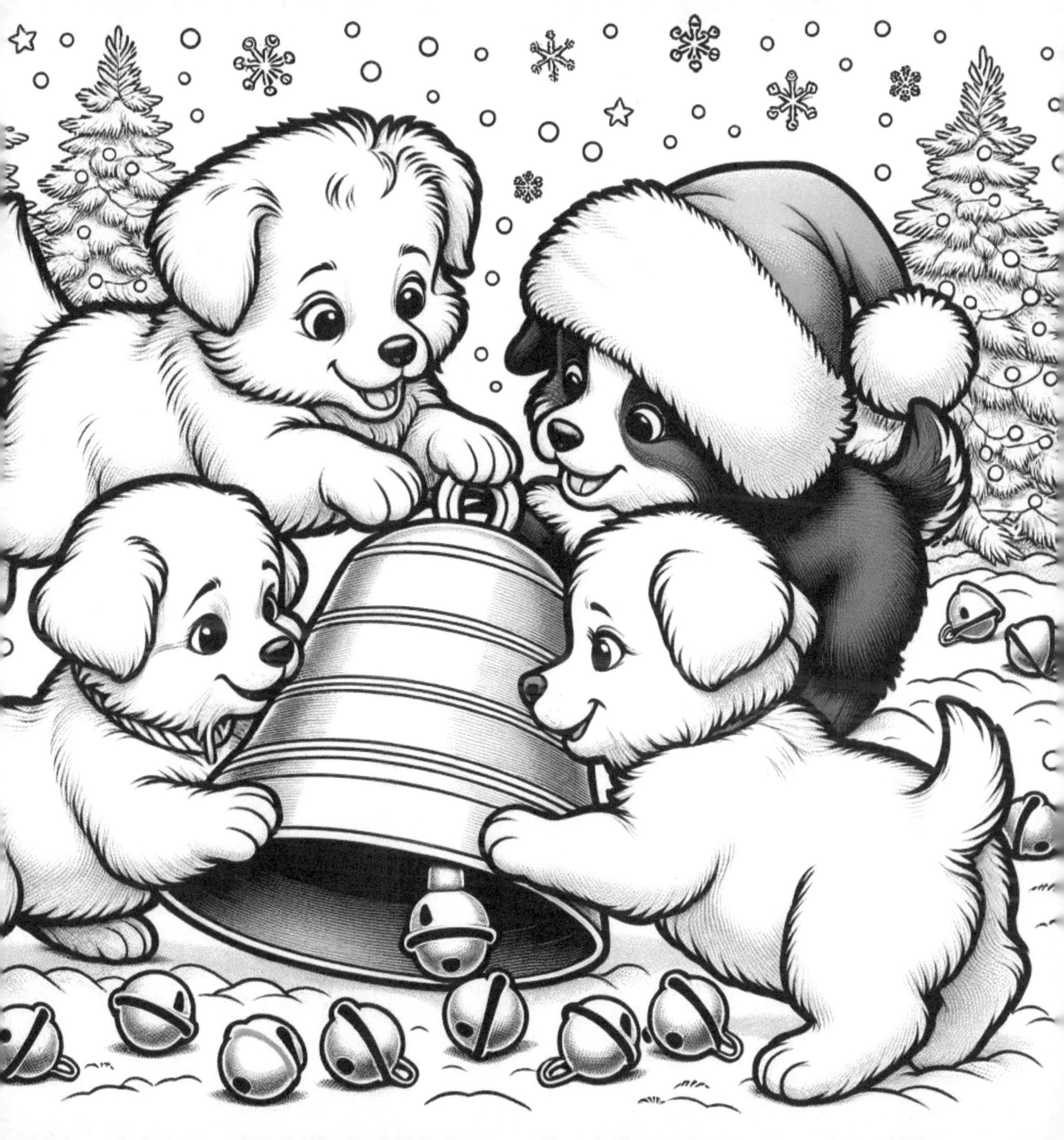

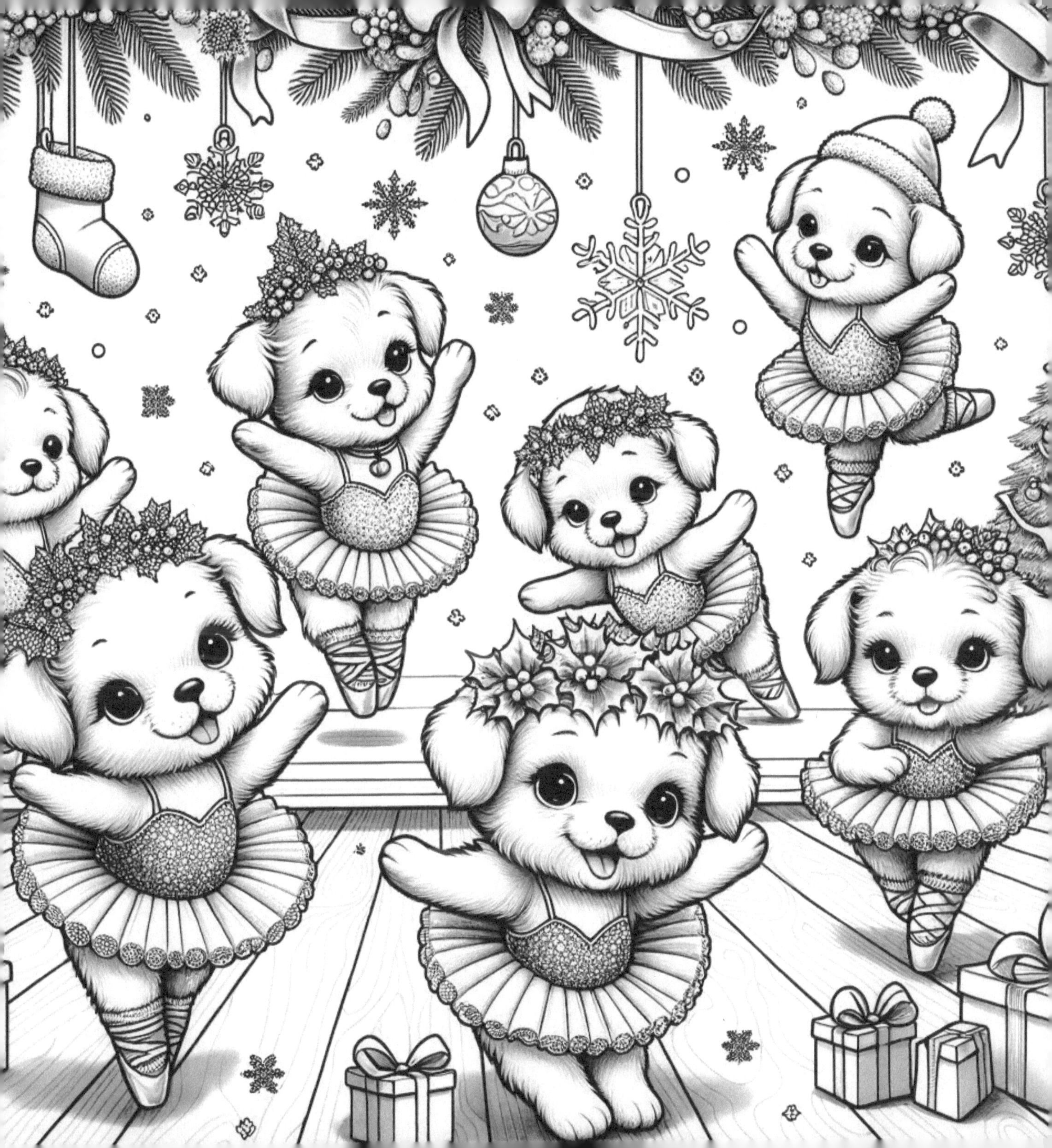

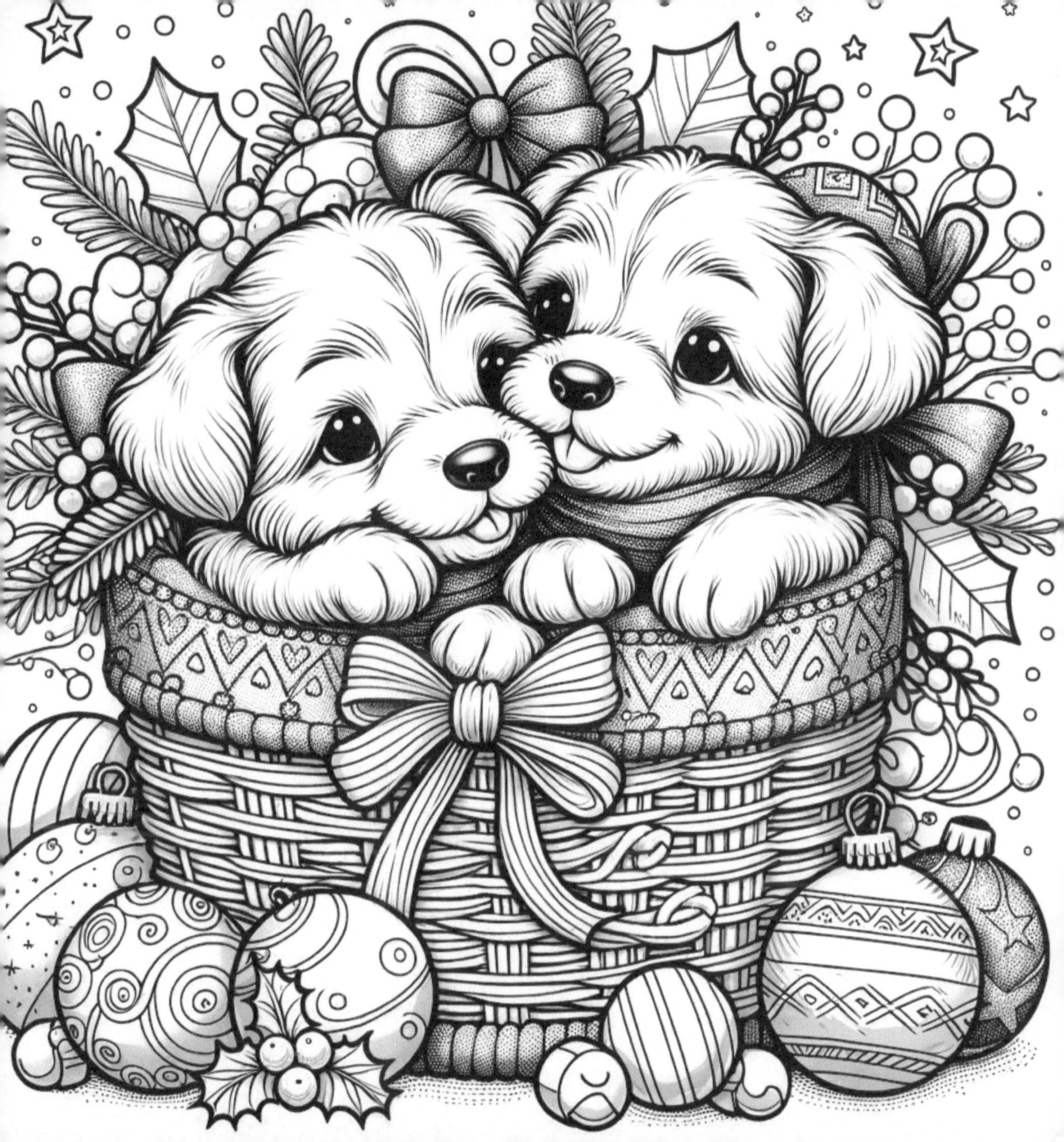

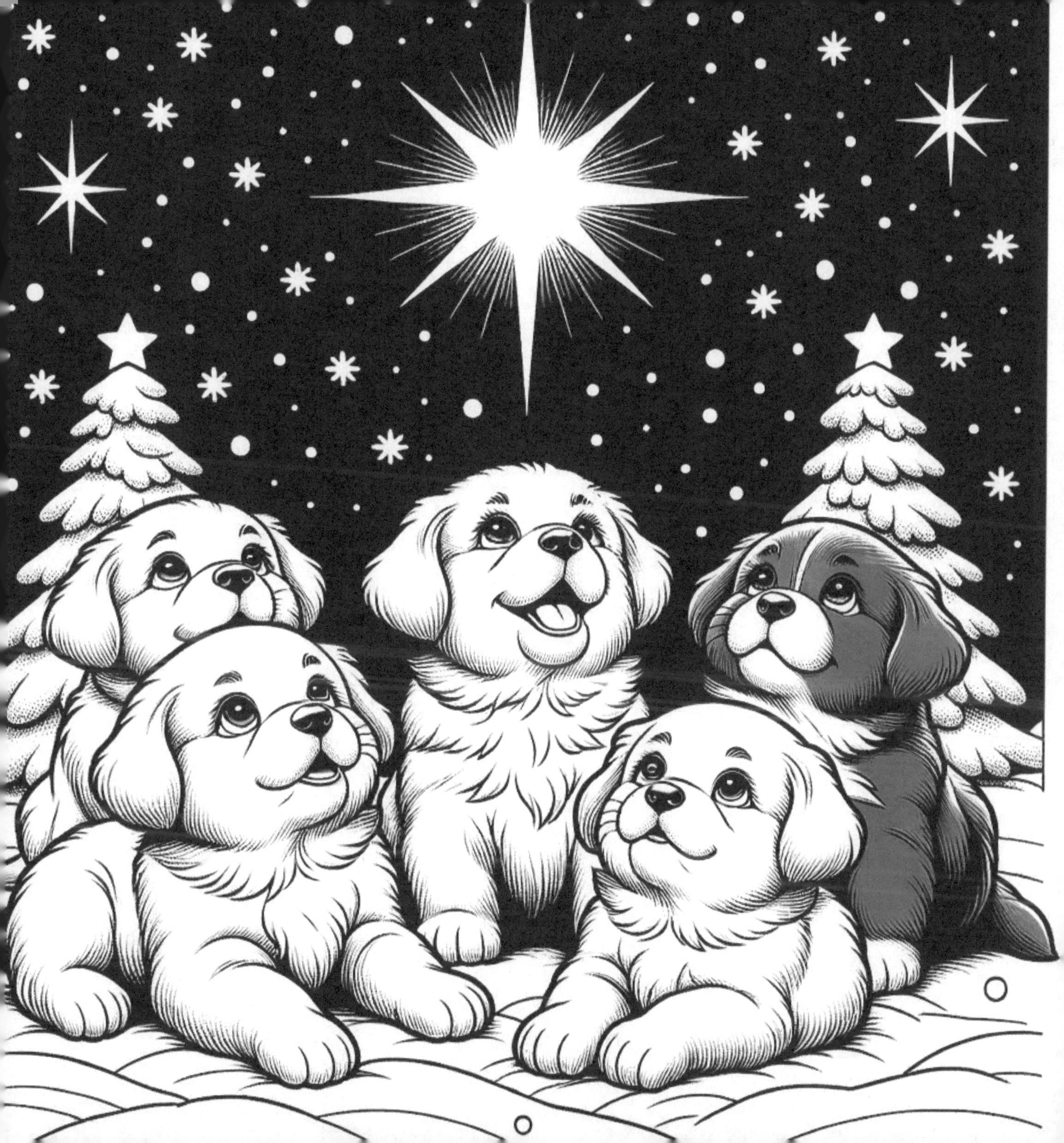

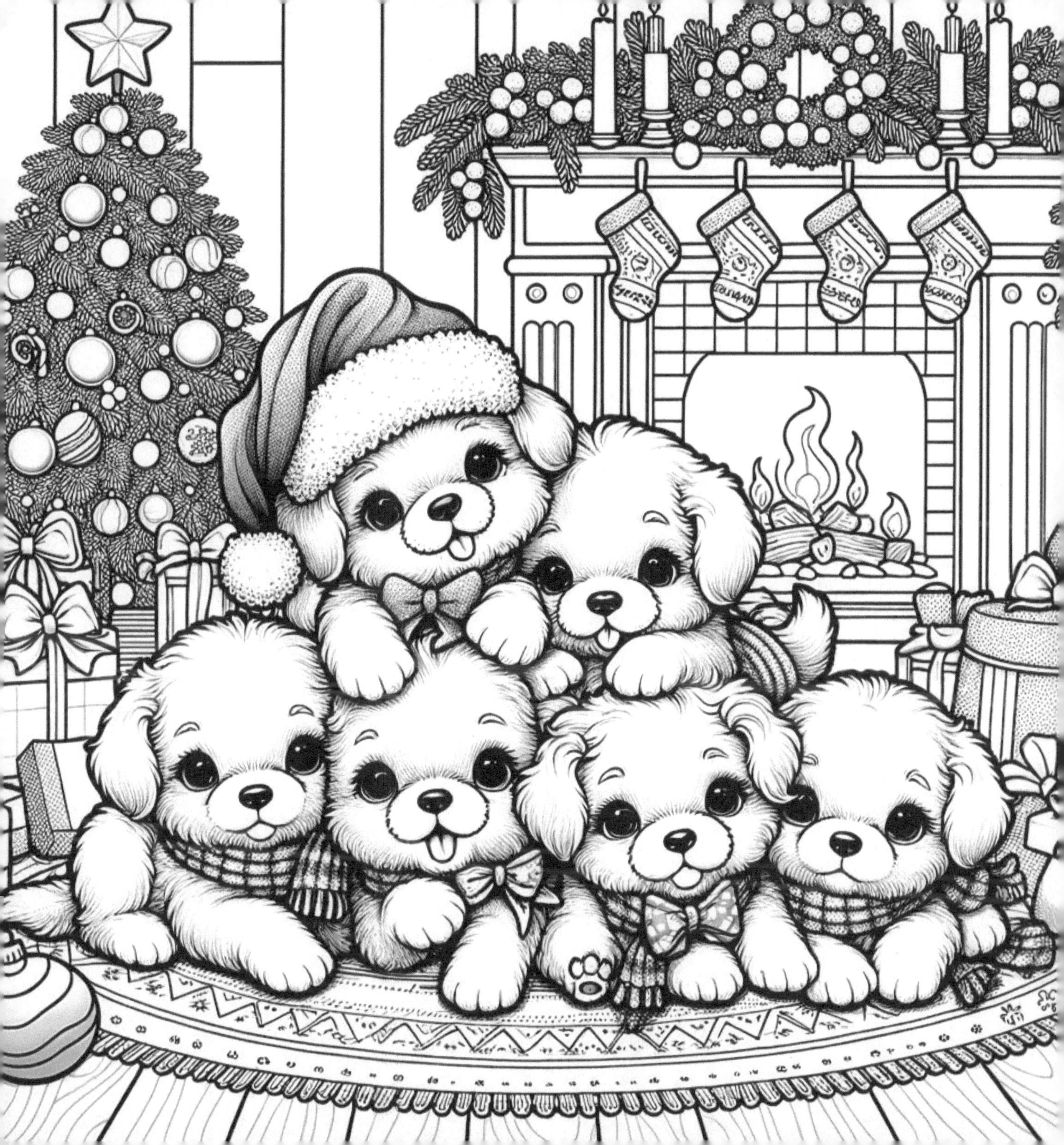

Made in United States
Troutdale, OR
12/22/2024

26997351R00033